I wish I'd said that too!

I wish I'd said that too!

An Anthology of Witty Replies
collected by
Kenneth Edwards

Abelard · London

ISBN 0 200 72529 7 (hardback)
ISBN 0 200 72528 9 (paperback)

Abelard-Schuman Limited
A Member of the Blackie Group
450 Edgware Road
London W2

Printed in Great Britain by
Robert MacLehose & Co. Ltd
Printers to the University of Glasgow

May I have tomorrow off, sir? I should like to attend my mother-in-law's funeral.

So should I.

A local soap-manufacturer plastered the town, at great expense, with posters which read 'Buy X's soap.' Overnight, someone added 'If you can't get Y's.'

A bishop who had just had new dentures made for him was invited by the dentist to look in the mirror. He did so, and immediately exclaimed, 'Christ!', then again at the top of his voice, 'Christ!'. Shocked and dismayed, the dentist asked what was wrong. The bishop turned to him, beaming. 'Wrong, my boy?' he said. 'Nothing's wrong. Owing to your skilled work, I can now, for the first time in ten years, pronounce the name of Our Lord without whistling.'

An elderly cockney woman was telling a friend about an altercation she had had with a neighbour.

'And what did you say then?' asked the friend.

'I kep' me dignity,' was the reply. ' "Pig" I ses, and swep' out.'

'But apart from that, Mrs Lincoln, what did you think of the play?'

A lady pianist who had just completed an indifferent performance addressed the young man who had been turning the pages for her:
'I hope you didn't notice the false note?'
Young man, doing his best to be gallant:
'Which one?'

'Isn't your dress a little young for you, dear?'
'Do you think so, dear? I think yours suits you perfectly. It always has.'

An American in a London restaurant had started eating what he had taken to be some kind of Scandinavian cheesecake, but which was in fact a sausage roll which had outstayed its welcome, and had begun to emit an unpleasant smell. The American looked round wrathfully and caught the eye of the head waiter, who hurried up to ask what was wrong.
'See here,' growled the American, pointing to his plate, 'something's died in my bun.'

Small child to unattractive male visitor: 'I wanted to see you specially, cos mother said you were a self-made man.'

'So I am, my dear, so I am. And proud of it.'

'But—but why did you make yourself look like that?'

'What do you have when you wake in the morning?'
'A roll in bed with honey.'

Napoleon was explaining to one of his marshals before a battle exactly what his plan of action was. 'If my orders are obeyed to the letter,' he added, 'we shall win the day.'

'God willing, sire.' said the marshal piously. 'God has nothing to do with it,' growled Napoleon.

'I'm going to give you a piece of my mind.'
'Not too large a piece! You can't spare it.'

The young student of Physics had done very badly so far in his oral examination. 'I'll give you one more chance,' said the examiner. 'What is electricity?' The student clutched his forehead desperately. 'I'm terribly sorry, sir,' he said. 'I knew when I got up this morning, but now it's completely slipped my mind.' 'I see,' replied the examiner, 'This is a much more serious matter than you seem to realise. This morning only two persons knew what electricity is: God Almighty and yourself. And now you've forgotten.'

Guide to a coach full of North country tourists. 'We shall soon be passing one of the best known and most picturesque pubs in Sussex.' Voice from the back of the coach—'Why?'

'I buried my husband three months ago.'
'Oh, I'm sorry, what was wrong with him?'
'He was dead.'

Door to door salesman: 'Good morning madam, is your husband in?'
'No, come inside.'

'Are you a virgin?'
'Not yet.'

Post office clerk to old lady posting a parcel containing a Bible.
'Anything breakable in it, Ma'am?'
'Only the Ten Commandments.'

Robert Menzies, while speaking at a political meeting, was interrupted by a woman who shouted—
'I wouldn't vote for you if you were the Archangel Gabriel!'
'If I were the Archangel Gabriel, madam,' replied Menzies, 'you would scarcely be in my constituency.'

A number of warships under the command of an admiral entered harbour, and one of them tied up in so sloppy a fashion that its captain expected a blistering reproof from the flagship. Sure enough, a signal was received from the flagship, but to the captain's astonishment it contained only the word 'good'.
Convinced that there must be some mistake he queried the message, whereupon a second signal was received from the flagship which read: 'amendment to my first signal: after "Good" insert "God".'

When David Niven was an Army Officer he was obliged to listen to a long and boring address by a visiting general. When the lecture was finally over, the general asked whether anyone had any questions. 'Yes,' replied Niven, 'what's the time? I have a train to catch.'

The spiritual jurisdiction of the Bishop of Fulham is not confined to the see of Fulham, but extends to all Anglicans living in South-West Europe. One day the Bishop, on a visit to Rome, sought and was granted an audience with the Pope.

'It is very good of your Holiness to receive me,' he said.

'Not at all,' replied the Pope. 'After all, I have the honour (have I not?) to be in your Lordship's diocese.'

London taxi-driver to woman motorist, whose car had nearly grazed his own. 'Do you think you own the * road?'

Woman motorist: 'I've got the same * right to the * * road as you have.'

Taxi driver: 'Sorry, lady.'

'No, Salome dear, not in the fridge, please.'

A Frenchman arrived wearing a lounge suit at a party where everyone else was in evening dress. The hostess, seeking to put him at his ease, welcomed him effusively and said how glad she was that he had been able to come. 'Alas, Madame,' he replied, 'I apologise that I come not in my nightdress.'

Muddle-headed old gentleman : 'Let me see, young man, was it you or your twin brother who was killed in the war?'
Young man, with heavy sarcasm : 'It was me, sir.'

'Goodness, Mae,' said a friend of Mae West, 'where did you get those beautiful pearls?' 'Never mind,' replied Mae, 'but you take it from me that goodness had nothing to do with it.'

A self-styled philosopher of the 18th century, who was notorious for not returning books lent to him, was accustomed to say that he was concerned solely with things of the mind and took no interest in such sordid matters as commerce.
'Nevertheless,' replied one of his friends, 'there is one branch of commerce for which you are ideally fitted.'
'And what is that?' enquired the philosopher.
'Book-keeping.' replied his friend.

A very old lady was visiting a Motor Show, and asked one of the young salesmen to explain to her how a motor-car worked. The young man plunged into an elaborate account of the internal combustion engine, touching on the function of the carburettor, the sparking plugs, the pistons, the gears etc. The old lady nodded intelligently at intervals, and when the young man finished she thanked him and said with a beaming smile, 'And now tell me, where do you light the fire?'

During the First World War a mounted officer encountered an exhausted column of infantry. 'I say, are you the West Riding?' he asked. Voice from the ranks: 'No, we're the ruddy Buffs—walking.'

'You're very affectionate today, George. Is there any special reason?'
'Well, Mildred, the truth is that my secretary doesn't understand me.'

A non-conformist pastor was a strong prohibitionist and had a large placard erected outside his chapel which read—
'Drink is your enemy!' Overnight someone added the words, 'Love your enemies!'

At a formal dinner-party Lord Birkenhead refused the last course and instead produced a cigar, bit off one end, and asked his hostess if he could have a light. She nodded to the butler, who provided one, and then said icily: 'I hope, Lord Birkenhead, you don't mind our eating while you smoke?'

'What is a widower?'
'The husband of a widow.'

While Drury Lane Theatre, the uninsured property of Richard Sheridan the playwright, was being destroyed by fire, Sheridan himself was seen sipping wine in a nearby coffee-house. One of those who saw him exclaimed at his unnatural calm, but he replied that there was surely nothing unnatural in a man taking wine at his own fireside.

Winston Churchill was once asked what he thought of democracy as a system of government. 'I think it's the worst there is,' he said, and then added thoughfully, 'except for all the others.'

'Tell me one of the symptoms of advancing age.'
'Getting a "morning after" without having had a "night before".'

When British troops were still stationed in Egypt, a car containing King Farouk and two of his aides, one of which was driving, collided with, and damaged beyond repair, an empty Army sentry box. At the subsequent enquiry, the only British witness of the incident, a sergeant, was required to give evidence. 'Sir,' he said, addressing the presiding officer, 'I was on duty outside B Block yesterday morning when I seen a car containing three wogs—' At this point the presiding offcer interrupted to say that he could not allow His Majesty the King of Egypt to be described as a 'wog' and that the witness must rephrase his evidence accordingly. 'Beg pardon, Sir,' said the sergeant. 'I should'a said that I was on duty yesterday morning outside B Block when I witnessed the approach of a car containing 'is Majesty the King of Egypt and two other wogs.'

Little girl encountering stranger in the sitting room—
'Who are you?'
'I'm your uncle on your mother's side.'
'Oh well, if you knew as much about mother as I do you'd jolly well be on father's side.'

An American senator was to deliver an address at an American University on graduation day, and was racking his brains in an effort to think of something original to say. It was not until he reached the swing-doors of the Assembly Hall in which he was to speak, that inspiration came to him. For on the brass plates attached to each of the swing-doors was inscribed the word 'push'. The senator duly entered the hall, mounted the rostrum and delivered his address, which differed little from other such addresses, but before concluding he said:

'There is one thing which everyone who wants to get ahead in this great country of ours needs more than anything else; and if you ask me what it is, I reply that it is inscribed upon the doors of this very hall.'

All the young graduates immediately craned their necks to see what was written on the swing-doors. It was the one word—'pull!'

Visitors to ducal mansion—'Are their Graces at home?'

Cockney footman—' 'Is is. 'ers ain't.'

Mother: 'Now Johnny's going to Grammar School I think we ought to buy him an encyclopaedia.'

Father: 'Nonsense, let him walk, same as I had to at his age.'

A clergyman, obliged to be absent from his parish for a while, arranged for his place to be taken by a *locum tenens*. One day during his absence, a lady called at the vicarage and asked to see the vicar. The door had been opened to her by the vicar's small daughter who replied, 'I'm afraid Daddy's away, but you can see the local demon if you like.'

Bernard Shaw, when asked whether he would appreciate the inclusion of his name in an Honours List, is said to have replied that to be Bernard Shaw was a sufficient honour for any man.

A former Archbishop of Canterbury, on his arrival in New York, was besieged by reporters asking for his views on every imaginable question, especially that of New York night-clubs. Thinking to avoid answering this potentially embarrassing question, the Archbishop decided to ask one in return, and enquired jocularly: 'Are there any night-clubs in New York?' But the Press had the last word, for on the morrow one of the papers had a headline which read—

' "Are there any night-clubs in New York?" Archbishop's first question on landing.'

Grocer: '*That two pounds of beef you sent me the other day was under weight. It weighed only* 1¾ *pounds.*'
Butcher: '*That's funny. I weighed it with two of your one pound packets of tea.*'

'When you and your wife quarrel, does she get hysterical?'
'Worse, she gets historical.'

'*How would you like your hair cut, sir?*'
'*In perfect silence, please.*'

Maid, asked why she had taken so long to go to the shops and back explained that the man who was following her had walked very slowly.

'*I met my young nephew for the first time today.*'
'*What's he like?*'
'*Very short, nearly bald, red-faced, clean-shaven and a hard drinker.*'
'*Good heavens! How old is he?*'
'*About six months.*'

Three men very much the worse for drink arrived at a railway station and asked when the train for London was due in. 'It's already arrived,' said the ticket-collector, 'and you'll have to look sharp if you want to catch it; it's just about to start.' The men were obviously so incapable that the ticket-collector bundled two of the men into the train when it had already begun to move, but the third man was left behind. 'I'm sorry we didn't get you on board as well, sir,' apologised the ticket-collector. 'Not half so sorry as my two friends will be,' replied the man, 'they came to see me off.'

'Most editors are failed writers.'
'Maybe, but so are many writers.'

'Can you play the violin?'
'I don't know; I've never tried.'

Winston Churchill, speaking at a political meeting, was interrupted by a woman who shouted: 'If you were my husband, I'd give you poison.'
'If I were your husband,' replied Churchill, 'I'd take it.'

'What are you complaining about? You married me for better or worse.'

'Well, the worse is much worse than I expected.'

Nervous passenger to air hostess: 'How often do aircraft of this type crash?'

Air hostess: 'Only once.'

Sales girl at the perfume counter of a big store to woman customer:

'What kind of perfume had you in mind, Madam?'

Customer, involuntary mother of fifteen children: 'Well, I suppose what I really need is a repellant.'

It has been said that on the occasion of a Coronation procession those escorting the Royal Coach on foot became aware that some kind of altercation was going on between its two occupants, one of whom, the female occupant, appeared to be exhorting her male companion to respond more cordially to the cheers of the crowd. Eventually the latter raised his voice and the following words were clearly heard. 'If you don't stop badgering me I shall get out and walk.'

A notice announced a forthcoming lecture on schizophrenia. Somebody added: 'I've half a mind to come.'

Diminutive hospital nurse (in response to mugger's demand for money): 'You can't intimidate me. Why, I've washed bigger men than you!'

Policeman to victim of assault: 'Can you describe your assailant?'

' 'Course I can. That's what I was doing when he hit me—describing 'im.'

Horatio Bottomley, sometime journalist, newspaper owner and aspirant to the Premiership, was eventually disgraced and sent to prison, where a visiting friend saw him sewing mail-bags 'Hullo,' said the friend, 'Sewing?' 'No,' said Bottomley, 'reaping.'

Workman, dissatisfied with the contents of his wage-packet: 'Well, strike me pink!'

Communist agitator: 'Go the whole hog, mate. Turn red.'

A young candidate for a Naval cadetship was undergoing an examination in General Knowledge. 'Tell me,' said the examiner, 'what animals eat fish?' The candidate stared at him incomprehendingly but said nothing. 'Come,' said the examiner, 'that's not such a difficult question is it? What about cats? What about penguins?' 'Oh, animals,' said the candidate. 'I thought you said admirals!'

'My curate was saying that he has not seen you at church lately.'

'No, well you see, it does so cut into one's Sundays.'

Harold Macmillan, commenting on a story that Harold Wilson, when a child had had to go to school without boots on, said that if this was so it was probably because his boots were too small for him.

Ernie Bevin and Aneurin Bevan were both distinguished members of the post war Labour administrations, but there was little love lost between them. Hearing Bevan described as 'his own worst enemy' Bevin was heard to mutter: 'not while I'm around.'

Psychiatrist: 'What's the trouble?'
Patient: 'It's my memory, doctor. I forget everything.'
Psychiatrist: 'And when did this trouble begin?'
Patient: 'What trouble?'

Victorian lady of the house reproachfully to newly engaged Irish maid: 'Do you know, Bridget, I can actually write my name in the dust on the piano.'

Bridget: 'Faith, ma'am, it's more than I can do. Sure, there's nothing like education after all!'

Lord Robert Cecil, an enthusiastic supporter of the League of Nations had been on a lecture tour in the USA and, on his return, was asked by his friends how he had been received. 'Kindly,' he replied, 'always kindly. But usually much too solemnly. The only exception was when the chairman of the meeting introduced me with the following words:

"Lord Robert Cecil has been described as a man with two long legs and an idea. I now call upon him to use the first to elevate himself and the second to elevate us".'

'When's the next train to Dublin, porter?'
'I'm sorry, sir, but the next train to Dublin left ten minutes ago.'

Between the two wars, at a very formal banquet, a loquacious lady found herself sitting next to a Chinese gentleman. Assuming from his lack of conversation that he had only a rudimentary knowledge of English, the lady relapsed into a monologue in pidgin English, which her companion seemed to understand perfectly, since, although he said nothing—he was not given a chance—he continually nodded and smiled in all the right places. She was still in full spate when the toastmaster 'prayed silence' for his Excellency the Chinese Ambassador, whereupon the Chinese gentleman rose to his feet and delivered an excellent speech in faultless English. During the applause which followed, he bent down and whispered in the lady's ear: 'Likee speechee?'

Barrister, commenting on a judge's summing up:
'Your Lordship puts the arguments so much more succinctly than I could.'
'I'm sure you don't really mean that, Mr. X.'
'No, my Lord, but it is customary to say it.'

An Irishman had been given a job which involved his catching a bus at 8.30 a.m. He had no watch, but a nearby church clock showed 8.30 when he boarded the bus. Some minutes later, however, he espied another church clock which showed 8.20. 'Mother of God,' he exclaimed, 'I'll have to get off. I'm travellin' in the wrong direction.'

Bishop, asked whether he would be free to attend a meeting of the Mothers' Union on a certain date, began turning over the pages of his diary. 'With the utmost disappointment,' he replied, 'I find that I shall.'

Irate traveller to porter at Irish railway station: 'You've got four clocks at this station and every damned one of them tells a different time!'

Porter: 'Well, sir, what 'ud be the point of havin' four clocks if they all showed the same time?'

John Barrymore, the actor, was asked by a reporter whether acting was as much fun for him as it used to be. 'Young man,' replied Barrymore, 'I am 75. *Nothing* is as much fun as it used to be.'

Lady at railway station to porter: 'I've asked no less than four people the time of my train, and every one of them has given me a different answer!'

'Well, mum, what do you expect if you ask four different people?'

Oldest inhabitant to visitor: 'I'm 93, I'm in good 'ealth and I ain't got an enemy in the world.'

'That's a beautiful thought.'

'Yes, Ma'am. They're all dead and gone, thank God.'

Man accused of manslaughter to counsel, who has unexpectedly secured his acquittal.

'I can't thank you enough. I don't know what I should have done without you.'

'I do, I think. About five years.'

A young English lady who was attending a cocktail party at the Irish Embassy in Paris wanted to visit the Ladies Room before being shown into the room in which the party was being held. The only person to consult seemed to be the French footman who was announcing the names of the guests as they arrived, so she crept up to him and said in a low voice, 'Ladies Cloakroom?' The footman made no reply, but, turning to the host and hostess announced at the top of his voice, 'Mesdames, Mesdemoiselles, Messieurs, Mees Gladys Clockroom.'

'What's the new bo'sun like?'

'Tough. The sort that eats sardines without bothering to open the tin.'

The motorist had pleaded guilty to crashing the red lights. 'But,' he added, 'I think the court should take into consideration the fact that I have often stopped at the green lights when I didn't have to.'

Lloyd George, asked to define the political position of Sir John Simon, as he then was, replied that Sir John had been sitting on the fence for so long that the iron had entered into his soul.

A professor about to deliver a lecture was introduced to the audience in such glowing terms that, when he eventually rose to speak, he was acutely embarrassed.

'Ladies and gentlemen,' he said, 'I know now how a pudding must feel when treacle is poured all over it. Moreover, after such an introduction, I can't wait to hear what I have to say.'

A man telephoned a neighbour's house and asked to speak to his school-boy son. 'Hullo, Dad,' said the boy, 'what is it?'

'I want you to come home at once,' replied his father, 'to help me with your homework.'

At a time when an attack on this country by Napoleon was believed to be imminent, the Prime Minister, William Pitt, received a letter enclosing a long list of gentlemen who expressed their willingness to serve in the Army against Napoleon, subject only to the condition that they should not be sent abroad. 'Except, I presume,' said Pitt sardonically to his secretary, 'in case of invasion.'

The late Eammon de Valera, the principal architect and first President of the Irish Republic, was in the middle of a revolutionary speech when he was arrested and subsequently sent to prison for 12 months. Immediately after serving his sentence, he was asked by his supporters to speak again and began his speech with the words, 'As I was saying when I was so rudely interrupted . . .'

An Irishman was in a public house, celebrating the birth of a child to his sister, and as time went on and drink followed drink he became thoroughly muddle-headed. 'Was the child a boy or a girl?' enquired the barman. 'Faith,' said the Irishman, striking his forehead, 'I never thought to ask. I don't know whether I'm an uncle or an aunt!'

When the Labour Party came to power immediately after the war, some elderly, old-fashioned people feared a reign of terror such as had accompanied the French Revolution. One such, seeking consolation, asked a Conservative MP what he thought of the Labour Prime Minister, Clement Attlee.

'You need not upset yourself,' was the reply, 'he's nothing but a sheep in sheep's clothing.'

During the First World War comparatively little provision was made for the protection of the civilian population against air raids. 'What do you do during air raids?' asked one old cockney woman of another. 'Well,' was the reply, 'I usually runs about, myself. As my 'usband says, a moving target is more difficult to 'it.'

Before being admitted to Oxford University, Oscar Wilde, in common with other students in those days, was required to qualify in Ancient Greek and in the oral examination his examiners asked him to translate a passage from the Greek version of the New Testament. The passage chosen was one which related to the trial of Jesus by Pilate and after Wilde had correctly translated a dozen or so verses he was told that he need not read any more. 'Oh, please let me go on,' said Wilde, 'I want to know what happens.'

One of the country's leading humorists was asked for his views on the upbringing of young children. 'Well,' he said, 'if they show any signs of mis-behaviour, I simply say to them "this is my house and I'm bigger than you are!" '

A young man had got a Jewish girl into trouble and offered to marry her. Her parents thanked him, but said they would rather have a bastard than a gentile in the family.

The American James Whistler, before he became a famous painter, worked in a Government department in Washington. Reproved for being constantly late at the office, he replied: 'It is not I that arrive too late. It is the office that opens too early.'

Asked what she wore at night, Marilyn Monroe replied, 'Chanel No. 5.'

A young gigolo had married a rich, elderly woman. 'I think it's disgusting,' said one of the female guests at the wedding reception to another. 'Why, she's old enough to be his grandmother.'
'Come, dear,' replied the other. 'Don't be uncharitable. At least she's young enough to be his mother.'

A young man at a formal dinner party was seated next to his hostess—a very attractive woman—but could find nothing to say. Eventually she noticed that he was eating very little, and said, 'Why Mr X, you seem to have a very small appetite. Is anything wrong?'

'N-no,' stammered the young man, striving to be gallant, 'sitting next to you would spoil any man's appetite.'

At a meeting of the United Nations, Harold Macmillan, speaking on behalf of the United Kingdom, was interrupted by Mr Kruschev, who, in order to emphasise his disagreement, hammered on his desk with the heel of one of his shoes. 'I wonder,' said Macmillan, blandly addressing the interpreters, 'whether I could have that translated?'

A German Minister travelling in Israel visited a concert hall called the Mann Auditorium. Assuming that it had been named after the famous German author, Thomas Mann, he expressed his pleasure that the Israelis should be willing thus to honour a distingusished German. He was, however, told that the hall had been named, not after Thomas Mann, but after the American, Frederick Mann of Philadelphia. 'Did he ever write anything?' enquired the Minister. 'Yes,' was the reply, 'a cheque.'

An experienced doctor was taking a newly qualified one with him on his rounds with the object of teaching him the tricks of the trade. Their first patient, a man, was told to take certain pills three times a day and to cut down his smoking. The second patient, a woman, was told to take pills— the same ones as the first patient, and to cut down her drinking. The third patient, also a woman, was ordered to take the same pills as the other two and to give up all her church work.

At this point the newly qualified doctor, a little puzzled by the rapidity of his colleague's diagnoses and by the treatment he had prescribed, asked for an explanation. 'Well,' said the experienced doctor, 'It's mainly a matter of keeping your eyes open. The first case was easy: the patient's fingers were stained with nicotine and when I went into the kitchen to wash my hands, I saw masses of empty cigarette packets. In the second case, the kitchen contained a number of empty whisky-bottles. In all three cases the pills I prescribed were mild tranquillisers designed to have a purely psychological effect.' 'Yes,' said the newly qualified doctor, 'I understand all that, but why on earth did you tell the third patient to give up her church work?' 'Well,' replied the other, 'there I had a bit of luck— you may have noticed that I dropped my pencil. When I bent down to pick it up, I saw the vicar under the bed.'

A young Scotsman had taken a job in a factory and had obtained a room close by. He had to start work at 8.30, but, because the window of his room had no curtains, and he was too thrifty to buy any, he was frequently awakened much earlier than was necessary. He accordingly painted the panes of his window black and, in order to ensure that he woke up in time, bought an alarm-clock. All went well that night: he went to bed at 10 and was awakened by the alarm clock at 7.30. On the following night all went well, except that he kept waking during the night and had some difficulty in getting to sleep again. Eventually he awoke with the feeling that he was throughly rested and needed no more sleep, so he got out of bed and threw open the window. It was broad daylight and the clock of the nearby town hall showed 1.30. Good Heavens! He remembered now that he had omitted to wind the clock and set the alarm! Hurrying into his clothes, he rushed to the factory, found his foreman, and poured out his story. 'So,' said the foreman, 'you overslept today and that's why you're late. But where were you yesterday?'

'Why does a surgeon wear a mask during an operation?'

'Because, if he makes a mess of it, he will be able to pretend it wasn't him.'

'Is Miss X at home?'
'I don't know, Ma'am. I'll go and ask her.'

'When's the next train to Dublin?'
'Not for another hour and a half.'
'Och, I'll soon wait that!'

During the war an oculist was introduced to each of his neighbour's four sons, three of whom were in the army. The fourth, a good deal smaller than his brothers, explained that he had volunteered for the army, but had been rejected because of his eyes. 'But,' said the oculist, 'I remember testing your eye-sight a year or two ago and found that it was exceptionally keen. What has happened to it since?' 'Well,' was the reply, 'it's not my eyesight that's at fault, it's my eyes; they're too near the ground.'

Nye Bevan asked Harold Wilson whether it was true that he had been born in Yorkshire. 'Not just born, Nye,' replied Wilson grandly, 'forged.' 'Really,' replied Bevan, 'I always thought there was something counterfeit about you.'

'What can I do to reduce my weight, doctor?'
'Follow my instructions to the letter and I'll expect three-quarters of you back in three months for a check up.'

G. K. Chesterton, the writer and poet, was one of the fattest men in England, and found it impossible to squeeze through a narrow doorway. 'Try it sideways, Mr Chesterton,' suggested someone. 'I have no sideways,' replied Chesterton.

'*Good Heavens, Jeeves. Is there anything you don't know?*'
'*I could not say, sir.*'

A rather weedy little man and his large wife attended a fancy dress ball as Henry IV of France and a Norman peasant respectively. The little man, having whispered to the butler announcing the guests who he and his wife were, and what they were supposed to represent, the man bellowed: 'Mr and Mrs X as King Henry the Fourth of France and an enormous pheasant.'

A conceited young man attending a dinner party in company with Dr Johnson, was so unmannerly as to taunt the old gentleman.
'*Tell me, Doctor,*' *he said,* '*what would you give to be as young and sprightly as I am?*'
'*Why sir,*' *said Johnson,* '*I should almost be content to be as foolish and conceited.*'

A lady in an advanced stage of pregnancy was approached by the village gossip who said: 'Excuse me, but are you going to have a baby?' 'Oh no,' replied the other drily, 'I'm just carrying this around for a friend.'

'Tell me, children, what is the main use of cow hide?' Dead silence, then one arm shot up. 'Please, miss, to hold the cow together.'

A gentleman who had spent two months at a mountain hotel had put on a good deal of weight. 'Do you know,' he said to the manager, 'I'm glad I came here. The place seems to agree with me.'

'Yes, indeed, sir,' replied the manager. 'Why, you're twice the gentleman you were when you first came here.'

A newly commissioned, very pompous young officer was holding forth to some of his fellow officers in the mess about what was to be expected of an officer and a gentleman, etc., etc. His companions were bored to death, and were all relieved when he looked at his watch, rose, and said, 'Well, it's getting late. I'm going to bed. Good night, gentlemen.'

'Goodnight, officer,' replied one of them.

'How is it, Bridget, that every time I come into the kitchen I find you reading instead of getting on with your work?'

'I think it must be those rubber soled shoes you've taken to wearing, Mum.'

A workman was trying to explain the principle of adult suffrage to one of his mates. 'Listen, Bill. One man, one vote. Can't you understand that?' But Bill still looked blank.

'Let me put it this way, then,' said his mate. 'One bloody man, one bloody vote!' Understanding slowly dawned in Bill's face— 'Well,' he said, 'why didn't you bloody say so before?'

A father, the head of a family business, was anxious that his son should follow in his footsteps and in due course succeed him. His son was all for it, and, after going through the form of working in various junior posts, started giving orders in all directions, frequently exceeding his authority. Eventually his father sent for him and told him he was taking too much on himself. 'But father,' said the young man, 'you told me you wanted me to follow in your footsteps.' 'Yes,' replied his father, 'but please give me time to get out of them first.'

'What a charming girl!'
'Yes, but I'm afraid she has a past ahead of her.'

A very up-and-coming estate agent was telephoned mistakenly by a lady wanting maternity garments. 'I'm afraid you've got the wrong number, Madam,' he said, 'but can I interest you and your husband in a larger house?'

A small boy was attending, with his mother, an exhibition of abstract painting. 'This picture,' she told him, 'is supposed to be a cowboy and his horse.' 'Well,' replied the boy, 'why isn't it?'

A lady attending an exhibition of abstract paintings, was contemplating an exceptionally painful specimen. Asked what she thought of it she replied: 'I've often suffered from migraine, but this is the first time I've seen a picture of it.'

'This is not a smoking compartment, madam, but would you mind my lighting a cigar?'
'Not if you don't mind my being sick.'

A young lady-killer was making amorous advances to an attractive waitress without much success. Eventually, when she had brought him his bill, he made one last attempt .'Are you sure,' he cooed, 'that there aren't three little words that you'd like me to whisper into your ear?'

'Yes,' was the reply. 'Keep the change.'

A patient who complained of feeling constantly tense, irritable and on edge, was given some tranquillising pills, and, after an interval was asked whether she felt any better. 'No,' she replied, 'I feel just the same. But I find that other people behave much better. They're more relaxed, less provoking, more considerate.'

Old lady to verger: 'Could you please find me a place near the pulpit?'

'Certainly, madam. Do you find it difficult to hear unless you sit in the front of the Church?'

'Yes, it's because of the agnostics. They're terrible in this church!'

Wife to husband at cocktail party. 'George, you mustn't drink any more.'

'Why ever not? I'm perfectly sober.'

'No, you're not. Your face is getting blurred already.'

A school teacher, Miss X, married Mr Y in term time, and got a friend, Miss Z, to take over her job while she was away. Later, at a party, the hostess was about to introduce Mr Y to Miss Z when he intervened with the words,

'Oh, Miss Z and I are old friends. She took my wife's place during my honeymoon.'

Just as a transatlantic liner was putting out to sea, a young woman fell overboard, and was heard to scream that she couldn't swim. Seconds later, to the astonishment of all present, an elderly man of over 70, went hurtling after her and eventually, amid rousing cheers, brought her to safety. Such was the admiration felt for the old man's heroism that a banquet was held in his honour at which the Captain of the ship made a speech, and, amid the applause which followed, the old man was urged to reply. He accordingly rose and said, 'I've only one thing to say. Who pushed me?'

A bulky woman entered an omnibus in which all the seats were occupied. 'Well,' she said belligerently, 'isn't some gentleman going to offer me his seat?' A little man rose. 'I'm willing,' he said, 'to make a contribution.'

A pretty faced young school boy was asked whether he minded having to wear spectacles. 'No,' he said, 'it stops the other boys from fighting me and the girls from kissing me.'

Groucho Marx, asked whether he knew what an extravaganza was, replied: 'I ought to. I married one.'

Three old gentlemen, aged respectively 70, 80, and 90, were discussing the best way to die. 'I should like to die instantaneously in a car accident,' said the one aged 70. 'I should like to die instantaneously in an air crash,' said the one aged 80. 'You boys have no ambition,' said the one aged 90, 'I should like to be shot by a jealous husband.'

'Your uncle is a bit of an old playboy, isn't he?'
'Yes, but he only chases girls now if it's downhill.'

'My boy, whoever marries my daughter will gain a prize of inestimable value.'
'Would you mind showing me the prize, sir?'

Some male and female teenagers were shown the sentence—'Woman without her man is a savage,'and asked how it should be punctuated. The boys said it required no punctuation, but the girls punctuated it thus—

'Woman! Without her, man is a savage.'

A young American of sixteen was to attend a public school in England and was being interviewed by his prospective headmaster.

'Have you any questions?' asked the head.

'Well, yes, sir,' answered the boy. 'Is smoking allowed?'

'I'm afraid not.' said the head.

'Is alcoholic liquor allowed?'

'No, I'm afraid that isn't allowed either.'

'How about dates?'

'Well,' said the head, a little puzzled, 'dates are all right provided you don't eat too much of them.'

An Irish husband was being prosecuted for assaulting his wife, but the wife refused to testify against him. 'I'm content to leave him to God, my Lord,' she said. 'Oh, dear me, no,' said the judge. 'It's far too serious a matter for that.'

'Have you ever been to a psychiatrist?'

'Good Lord, no. Anyone who goes to a psychiatrist needs to have his head examined.'

Someone asked whether a recently deceased friend, reputedly a miser, had left any money. 'Him leave money!' was the reply. 'He was taken from it!'

A would-be mountaineer, accompanied by an experienced guide, was climbing a rock-face and had reached a point at which it seemed too risky to climb any higher. He appealed to the guide, who agreed that the next step called for a good deal of courage and skill. 'It's up to you to decide whether you go any further.' he said. 'But if you do and lose your footing, remember to look to the right as you go down. The view is fantastic.'

'Daddy, where are the Alps?'
'Ask your mother; she's always putting things away.'

'Ten shillings or a fortnight,' said the Irish Magistrate to the drunk. 'Why your Honour, I've only two shillings in the world,' pleaded the man. 'Well, then, you must go to jail,' replied the magistrate. 'If you hadn't spent your money on getting drunk, you'd have been able to pay the fine.'

An elderly American and his wife were seeing the sights of Florence. They had seen most of them, but had still to visit the famous Ponte Vecchio. The wife was all for pressing on and urged her exhausted husband, who had collapsed on a convenient bench, to make the effort. 'Listen, honey,' he replied. 'I know the Ponte Vecchio's mighty old, and that we gotta see it. But if I sit here for half an hour it will be that much older when we *do* see it.'

An Englishman visiting an Irish stately home, pulled up at some lodge gates and was assured by the Lodge keeper that he had reached his destination. But before him stretched a drive which looked almost half a mile long and there was no sign of a house at the end of it. 'It's a very long drive, is it not?' the visitor asked the lodge-keeper. 'It is, your Honour,' replied the lodge-keeper. 'But if it was any shorter, it wouldn't reach the house.'

A man with an empty pipe in his mouth boarded a bus, and was told by the conductress that smoking was not allowed.

'I'm not smoking,' he replied.

'But you've got a pipe in your mouth,' said the conductress.

'I know I have: and I've got shoes on me feet, but I'm not walking!'

A small boy returned from school, his face disfigured with bruises and scratches. 'What on earth have you been doing?' asked his mother. 'Fighting?' 'Well, yes,' said the boy. 'It's all my own fault, really. I challenged Johnnie Smith to a duel, so I had to give the choice of weapons to him.' 'And what did he choose?' 'His big sister.'

'Tell me, my son, what must one do in order to be absolved from sin?'

'Please, father, one has to sin.'

A president of France was paying an informal visit to a mental home and one of the inmates whose hand he shook asked who he was: 'I have the honour to be President of the Republic,' he said. The inmate chuckled. 'You'll soon get over that,' he said. 'When I first came here, I thought I was Napoleon.'

An Irishman, applying for a job in a factory, was told that the factory was already over-staffed.

'Why,' he replied, 'the little bit of work I'd do would hardly be noticed.'

The congregation was dismayed when the lightning struck and sent rafters crashing down on the church altar.

'Fortunately,' said the vicar, 'we are insured against Acts of God.'

On her wedding day, Miss A spent hours on her appearance. She tried every beauty treatment, and was finally satisfied with the result. At the altar she joined her bridegroom, who looked at her and said; 'Who are you?'

There were four people in the doctor's waiting room when in walked a Pakistani. He was about to go straight into the surgery when a woman jumped up and grabbed his arm, saying in very deliberate English:

'We are before you. You take your turn, understand?'

The Pakistani, in equally deliberate English, replied: 'No, you are after me. Me doctor. Understand?'

'I understand he can speak five languages.'

'Yes, and can't say a word of sense in any of them.'

Sherry, the pet cat of the Bishop of A, has been renamed Shandy.

'One of my clergy suggested Sherry was a little too strong,' the Bishop explained.

An advertisement in a well-known paper ran:

'Wanted, hard-boiled candyman. Apply . . . Hotel.'

A reader commented:

'To take the place of one who was only half-baked, perhaps.'

A scientist told an audience during his lecture:

'150,000 germs can live on a pound note for years.'

'Good heavens,' said one listener, 'they're cleverer than I am, I can hardly do it for an hour.'

When Walter Pater had concluded his talk an enthusiastic group of friends gathered round to congratulate him. He hoped, he said, that the audience were able to hear what he said.

'We overheard you,' said Oscar Wilde.

Giving evidence in court, Miss A denied swearing at Miss D.
She told the court that she said to Miss D:
'Suppose you think I'm rich.'
However Miss D interpreted this as:
'Horsey-toothed bitch.'

A drunk staggered up to a railway ticket office and slurred,
'A return ticket, please.'
'To where, sir?'
'Back here, of course!'

A young poet, Mr Laman Blanchard, sent to Charles Dickens a contribution for inclusion in the publication Household Words. *The piece was entitled 'Orient Pearls at Random Strung'; but Dickens returned it with the comment:*
'Dear Mr Blanchard—too much string. Yours, CD'

It was reported that a Sydney man was so insensitive to pain that he would allow people to drive nails into him.
'Oh,' said one cynic, 'What's a man like that doing outside politics?'

The low-born wife of a multi-millionaire was doing her best to impress her guests.

'*I always make a point of keeping my jewellery clean,*' *she said.* '*For example, when my diamonds get dirty, I wash them in brandy.*'

'*Really?*' *said one of her guests,* '*What a bore that must be for you. When my diamonds get dirty, I just throw them away.*'

An officer said to a young corporal:

'Now supposing the patrol didn't return at the proper time, what would you do?'

The corporal gave the matter much thought, and then replied:

'Sell their kit, sir.'

A Yorkshireman stole a tin of salmon, the magistrates were told. When they asked why he did it, he replied:

'*I got fed up pinching spam.*'

Mr A was propped up in front of the television, beer bottle in one hand, cigarette in the other, while his wife looked on disapprovingly.

'But surely you don't imagine,' he said, 'that I *enjoy* being a Hedonist?'

A young man took his new girlfriend back to the door of her flat after an evening out.

'You're in luck,' she said. 'The rest of the week I'm liberated, but on Saturdays I revert to being a sex-object.'

St Peter stood by the doors of heaven, and welcomed the gentleman who came towards him:

'This is a very pleasant surprise,' said the man. 'As an atheist, I naturally expected to go to hell.'

A schoolboy, with a penitent expression, sat opposite the Headmaster.

'You realise,' said the Master, 'that failing your English O level means saying goodbye to your career as a T-shirt slogan-writer?'

The Scottish prisoner standing in the dock, said to the judge:

'I'd rather grass than sup porridge.'

Asked by Lord A to interpret this remark, the advocate translated:

'I would rather inform on my associates than partake of cuisine in Her Majesty's prison.'

Lady, on being introduced to an attractive blonde:
'I'm delighted to meet you. My husband has told me so little about you.'

An elderly woman was sitting in a squalid and untidy room, her hair in curlers and surrounded by beer bottles and debris. A middle aged man came in. 'Mother,' he said, 'shouldn't you be getting over your post-natal depression by now?'

A gang of raiders attacked a bank last week, but they were spotted by Mr A, who said:
'I saw five men in balaclavas, casually jogging along the pavement in single file. I thought that they were out for a gentle training run . . . except that they all had guns and pickaxe handles, and one had a sledgehammer.'

Reporting to Head Office, a country manager for a certain bank said: 'The purpose of the annual concert is that young people of the district should get together. The results of their efforts are sent to an orphanage.'

Two youths were standing on the street corner. One said to the other:

'That's the trouble with living in London. There's nowhere to run away to.'

Charles Howard published a very foolish book which he called *Thoughts*. One day, he went to a coffee house and there met an acquaintance, Samuel Foote.

'Have you read my *Thoughts*?' he asked Mr Foote.

'No,' replied the other, 'I am waiting for the second volume.'

'Why?' enquired the author.

'Because I have heard,' said Mr Foote. 'that second thoughts are better.'

A family of five were rushed to hospital, to have their stomachs washed out after the cat, with whom they had shared a meal of mushrooms, suddenly began to have stomach contractions. When they returned home weak and exhausted, the youngest went to look for the cat. Suddenly he came rushing back, crying, 'will we have kittens too?'

W. Somerset Maugham, the famous writer, during a discussion about Christian morals said:

'You know of course that the Tasmanians, who never committed adultery, are now extinct.'

Two women were sitting talking over the coffee cups: one said to the other, in a voice tinged with guilt.

'We pay our au pair practically nothing.'

Her friend answered: 'Why should you, dear, when the exchange rate is so much in her favour?'

Two catholic priests went to visit Lourdes together. On the way back one suddenly started leaping up and down excitedly.

'What *is* the matter?' asked the other.

'I'm cured,' replied the first. 'I'm cured of my totally illogical belief in religion!'

It was reported in a well known paper that an Irishman beat up a Jew because the Jews were responsible for the crucifixion. On being told that this event occurred 2,000 years ago he replied:

'But I only heard about it yesterday.'

A conversation was overheard between two prisoners. The first said to the second:

'Monday is out for a break, because I have to see my social worker; Tuesday they're showing a film I wouldn't want to miss; and Wednesday's my pottery lesson; . . .'

Two tramps were walking along by the side of the road together. One said to the other:

'I content myself thinking I've contributed nothing to this world, and it's a better place for it.'

To the question 'What is Greenwich mean time?' a Manchester boy replied:

'Greenwich mean time is absolutely the correct time, which we get from a place right down in the South of England, where the people can see the sun better than we can.'

H. J. Mincken who lived at the turn of the century, had his own rules for getting along.

'I've made it a rule never to drink by daylight,' he said, 'and never to refuse a drink after dark.'

An insurance broker tells of the time when he was examining a proposal for an import-export order. The letter from the insurers, on the other side of the world, asked:

'Do you want a cross liability?'

Puzzled, the broker asked: 'What's a cross liability?'

'My wife,' a junior partner replied.

A well-known daily paper asked the question: 'Can a business man tell the difference between right and wrong?' to which came the unqualified reply—'certainly, if he's allowed two guesses.'

Samuel Rogers, the poet, used to receive many guests in his home, including Sydney Smith—whose witty remarks he was fond of repeating.

'At one time,' he recalled, 'When I gave a dinner, I used to have the candles placed all round the dining room, and high up, in order to show off the pictures. One day, I asked Smith how he liked the plan.'

'Not at all,' he replied. 'Above there is a blaze of light, and below nothing but darkness and gnashing of teeth.'

A lady in Birminghan reported that her house had been burgled four times in the previous three weeks.

Local police said: 'It looks as though even burglars are now feeling the effects of our housing shortage.'

At a party given for well-known political dignatories, the following remark was overheard:

'Of course we want this government to fall; but we don't want our dagger found in its back.'

Dr Johnson was being congratulated by a lady on the fact that his dictionary contained no 'naughty' words.

'And how do you know that, Madam?' replied Johnson, 'unless you have read all through it looking for them?'

The mother of three little boys, Richard aged 8, Willy aged 7 and Tommy aged 5, found the two older boys in tears and asked what was the matter.

'Last week at school,' replied the 8-year-old, 'they taught us how to give artificial respiration to people who've fallen in the water. Well, just now Tommy fell into that big puddle at the bottom of the garden, and every time Willy and I try to give him artificial respiration he gets up and walks away!'

During the war the complaint was made that Winston Churchill had not given the country enough spiritual guidance. When Churchill heard of this he was indignant. 'Since I became Prime Minister,' he said, 'I have appointed not less than six new bishops. What more do they want?'

The people on a certain bus wondered why it was travelling so fast late at night. Then the conductor said:

'We're nipping along sharpish to miss the cinema crowd.'

'Good Heavens, is that a photograph of me? I look like a monkey!'

'You should have thought of that before letting yourself be photographed.'

A man who had several glasses too many at a cocktail party was making a childish exhibition of himself.

'Tell me,' said one of the women guests to his wife, 'what does your husband intend to be when he grows up?'

'No,' said a well-known comedian, *'you won't catch me
going to hospital after what happened to my mother there.'*
'Why, what happened to your mother in hospital?'
'I did.'

A doctor, who was also a biology lecturer, was
moving house. Among his possessions was a com-
plete plastic skeleton which could be taken to
pieces, bone by bone, and neatly packed into a
shallow box. This had to be handled gently for fear
of displacing its contents, and when the doctor's
wife saw one of the removal men about to hurl it
into the van, she cried out:

'Oh, be careful! Those are my husband's bones!'

Awestruck, the removal man sat down on the box
and reverently bared his head:

'I'm sorry, lady,' he said. 'I thought this was just
an ordinary removal. I didn't know it included a
funeral.'

*Mrs Amelia Earhart made her solo flight across the
Atlantic a little before Mrs Dionne of Canada gave birth
to quintuplets. Asked which achievement she considered the
greater, hers or Mrs Dionne's, she replied that she thought
Mrs Dionne, with sufficient practice, could do what she had
done, but doubted whether, however hard she practised, she
would ever be able to do what Mrs Dionne had done.*

During a period of drought a preacher summoned his congregation to attend a special service at which they would all pray for rain. When they were all assembled, he mounted the pulpit and addressed them sadly:

'Brothers and sisters,' he said, 'how can we ask the Lord for rain unless we have faith. I notice that none of you has brought an umbrella.'

A man who had spent a very convivial evening with some of his male friends decided to ring up his wife at 2 a.m. to tell her he would be home late.

'I hope I'm not disturbing you, dear,' he said when he got through to her.

'Oh, no,' replied his wife sarcastically. 'I had to get up in any case to answer the telephone.'

A preacher asked all those of his congregation who wished to go to Heaven to stand up. All rose except one man. Then he asked all those of them to stand who wanted to go to the other place. Nobody moved. Much puzzled, the preacher stared down at the non-co-operator. 'Where do you want to go?' he asked.

'Nowhere,' was the reply. 'I like it here.'

It was noticed that a young lady who normally wore glasses, never wore them in the presence of her boy-friend. Was this just vanity, she was asked?

'No,' she said, 'not entirely. Without my glasses I look better to George and he looks better to me.'

The boss's son had been taken into the firm in some unspecified capacity to 'learn the business from the bottom up'. Members of the junior staff were, however, uncertain how they stood with him and asked the manager for guidance.

'I'm glad you asked me that,' replied the manager, 'he's not to enjoy special privileges of any kind. Just treat him as you would anyone else who was due to take over the firm in a year's time.'

A man about to receive guests, was startled by the sight of his wife's new evening dress.

'Isn't that dress a little too revealing?' he asked.

'What of it?' his wife replied, 'is it me or my dress that our guests are coming to see?'

'Well,' replied her husband, 'whichever it is, they ought to be satisfied.'

A lady about to make a journey by air telephoned her husband's office from the airport.

'I'm afraid that Mr X is not available at the moment,' said his secretary, 'would you care to leave a message?'

'Yes,' said the wife, 'please tell him that I left in such a hurry that I failed to plug in the alarm on his side of the bed.'

'I'll tell him.' replied the secretary. 'May I ask who is speaking?'

A comparatively unknown young man stood for Parliament as an independent and, greatly to his surprise, found himself elected, having defeated the official Conservative candidate by a wide margin. Asked to account for his success, he replied:

'I think the only possible explanation is that all the people who knew me voted for the other fellow and all the people who knew him voted for me; and more people knew him than knew me.'

A little girl on her first day at boarding school was found by one of the mistresses in tears.

'What's the matter, dear?' asked the mistress. 'Are you home-sick?'

'No,' replied the little girl, 'I'm here-sick.'

On the first day of term the mistress of one of the junior classes asked her pupils whether any of them had done anything during the holidays to make someone else happy. After a pause, one of the little girls held up her hand.

'Yes, Joan?' said the teacher. 'What did you do?'

'Well,' said Joan, 'during the holidays I stayed part of the time with my aunt. She doesn't like me and when I left I am sure I made her happy.'

The French novelist Honoré de Balzac, liked wine, women and song, but seldom had enough money to pay for them. When, therefore, a rich uncle from whom he had expected nothing, died, leaving him a substantial sum, his elation knew no bounds, and, unable to keep still, he started throwing the furniture about. Before long one of his friends, who lived immediately below, came up to find out what was going on. De Balzac shouted,

'Congratulate me! At seven o'clock yesterday evening my uncle and I both passed on to a better life.'

A husband had been reproving his wife for spending too much.

'It's not me spending too much,' she retorted, 'it's you not earning enough.'

A student of sociology investigating juvenile delinquency decided to try and find out, at about 9 p.m., how many parents knew where their children were. Accordingly he telephoned ten couples to ask whether they knew where their children were. Eight of his calls were answered by children who did not know where their parents were.

The head of an American business firm was on vacation, but could not rid himself of his business worries. He accordingly cabled his office to ask whether all was well. The same day he received the following reply:

'Everything fine. Hope you are enjoying your vacation. We are.'

When questioned recently about allegations of poor service the GPO stated that they received only four complaints for every 100,000 calls they dealt with.

Presumably the others tried to convey their complaint by telephone.

Wife to husband who has just finished locking doors and closing windows before going to bed.

'Is everything shut up, dear?'

'That rather depends on you, dear,' was the reply.

A female hypochondriac was giving her doctor a long list of her ailments. When she had finished, he congratulated her.

'You must,' he said, 'have a magnificent constitution to be able to withstand all these onslaughts on your health.'

Someone was telling William Gladstone how much he admired a man who could stand up to his enemies.

'Standing up to one's enemies is commendable, no doubt,' replied Gladstone, 'but give me the man who can stand up to his friends.'

'Dear Mr Marx,' said a pushing woman journalist to Groucho Marx at a party. 'We met at Mrs X's. I'm sure you remember me?'

'I never forget a face,' replied Groucho, 'but in your case I'll make an exception.'

James Whistler, when asked by an aristocratic lady from Boston, where he had been born, gave the name of an insignificant town in Massachussets.

'Why, Mr Whistler,' said the lady in mock reproof, 'What possessed you to be born in a place like that?'

'The explanation is simple, Madam,' replied Whistler, 'I wished to be near my mother.'

A glamorous film star, touring a hospital full of wounded American soldiers, asked the occupant of the first bed she came to, whether he had killed any of the enemy.

'Yes, Ma'am,' replied the soldier. 'I shot one with a revolver, but not before he shot me and broke my right arm.'

Tenderly the actress bent down, kissed the man's right arm, and moved on to the next patient, of whom she asked the same question.

'Yes, Ma'am,' replied the patient. 'I killed one all right. I bit him to death.'

Winston Churchill was touring a part of London, which had been severely bombed the night before. Seeing one old cockney woman apparently in the best of spirits, he asked whether she had suffered much from last night's bombing.

'Nothing to speak of, sir,' she replied. 'There's one thing to be said for these air raids. They do take your mind off the war.'

A shop, badly in need of extra staff exhibited a notice saying:

'Sales assistant wanted; old or young; experienced or inexperienced; full time or part time; man or woman.' Overnight somebody had added the words:

'dead or alive.'